T0359137

SYDNEY
(EASTERN SUBURBS)

SYDNEY
HARBOUR

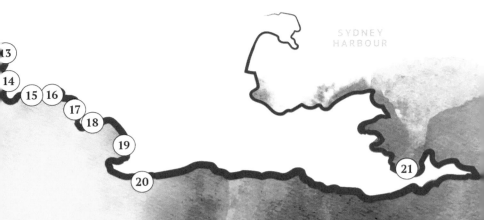

13

14

15 16

17

18

19

20

21

idyllic ocean
like a reader to a book
we bring our own meanings

LH

Coastal Poetry, first edition
Published by Pacific Ocean Press, 2023
Designed by Rosie Handley
Printed by Pegasus Print, Sydney
Type is set in PT Serif

ISBN 978-0-646-86476-1

COASTAL
POETRY

———

**BEACH & CLIFFTOP POEMS
FROM YARRA BAY TO WATSON'S BAY**

———

LIBBY HATHORN &
ELIZABETH CUMMINGS

FOREWORD

Libby Hathorn

When writer Elizabeth Cummings approached me with an idea for a coastal poetry collection, I was delighted. We both wanted to sing out about our astonishing Australian coastline; to sing out about our beaches, everything from the coastal walks and views to the wonder of beach and cliff side environments.

So we decided to make our very own collection of coastal poems from Yarra Bay to Watson's Bay. Having worked with Elizabeth in her role as head of the CBCA Eastern Suburbs Branch, I knew of her talent and tenacity.

We explored a different beach every few weeks, walked a bit, dreamed, observed and wrote. At each beach, through winter winds, through summer heat, we sat on Elizabeth's picnic blanket sometimes in rocky wet places, coffees in hand, took some photos, and wrote.

Where land meets sea has long been represented in art and literature; and as oceans rise and environments change we wanted to draw attention to our coastline and capture the precious here and now.

Elizabeth Cummings

When I moved to Sydney in 2008, I was struck by the beauty of the coastline. It was wild yet accessible, a completely different landscape to the northern hemisphere coastlines of my youth. It became my companion in the early days as a new migrant; a place of solace during times of grief and loss; and it continues to be the place where I run, swim and breathe in the beauty of this natural treasure.

Wanting to share this precious part of my life through poetry, I reached out to my dear friend and mentor, writer and poet, Libby Hathorn. Libby's genuine passion for the written word, especially poetry, and her childhood coastline experiences, made her the best woman to help guide this collection to its successful completion.

Over several months we met and walked and talked and laughed and listened to each other, to the natural world around us, and to that call deep inside us that demanded we sing out with grateful hearts and minds.

What has been accomplished is a shared collection of poetry, unique to a part of the magnificent Australian coastline.

Coogee Beach

ONTENTS

Deep Knowledge

The deep knowledge,
the tragedy, the displacement, the loss,
the crying out.
The wavering, the losing,
hard going.
The despair, the persistence,
hard going.
The claiming, the maintaining,
the naming, the saying and saying.
The pride, the language,
the saying and saying,
the name and the place.
The deep knowledge.

LH

To write these poems, we have traversed the land, the cliffs
and beaches of the Gadigal people of the Eora Nation.

With these poems we honour them and their land.

COASTLINE

Singing the Coast

All my life I've known you,
now to sing out what you mean,
from Yarra Bay to Watson's Bay
darling, the beaches in between.

I want to sing you Malabar,
Tamarama in your thrall,
ancient landscapes offered still
for surfers, walkers, dreamers all.

I want to sing you Little Bay,
Clovelly, Bondi Beach,
two miracles a day and more
sunrise, sunset on each.

And to the very edge of land
La Perouse at morning,
fresh and gutsy, cold and gusty
new understandings dawning.

Coogee and Maroubra Beach,
from wavelet to king tide
weaving boardwalks linked to each
sea grandeur by your side.

In blissful calm, in roiling storm
wherever I may die,
to the beaches of sweet Sydney
'My homing thoughts will fly!'

Sea Senses

I can lose myself and find myself
along Sydney's eastern coastal path.
And all before sunset.
Yarra Bay to Coogee, Bronte to Bondi,
Waverley Cemetery to Watson's Bay,
no matter where I begin, I am found
by expanses of water.
I see the Australian palette,
grey, brown and silver predominates.
I hear my heart and breath,
planes overhead and waves below.
I feel the wind, the gravel underfoot,
the sun beating down,
smell kiosk coffee and fried food.
Of all my senses, best of all,
I taste the freedom that comes
from being by the sea.

Coastal Boardwalk

You dip and curve, you swerve your way,
you pause and veer out yonder,
you track the earth but hug the edge
with rock face all asunder.
Now and then we stop and watch
waves' wild flagellations
or fix our gaze devoid of thought,
our sometimes consolations.
Just nature wild and sea surrounds
in all its moods and changes,
grateful walkers, sensual walks,
lifetimes of sea exchanges.

Of Oceans... and Love

As with love
I know the ocean is there
its high and low tides
governed by the emotional moon
waxing and waning
yet ever present.
In the blackest moments
where darkness holds court
it washes over me.
In the daybreak
cool, fresh, reborn
lapping or rushing
in foaming charges
it can knock me to the ground
grazing, choking, pinning me down
yet always I surface.
My skin prickles
at its first touch,
in the knowledge
of other times
when I have waded in
deeper and deeper
dipping below its glassy surface
I am enfolded, embraced
in a world of wonder.

Yarra Bay & La Perouse Headland

Looking Out from Yarra Bay

Construction spans the wharf
elephant AT-AT cranes loom large
overlooking children in Yarra Bay.
Aircraft overhead, stored cargo below
and stacked upon the wharf as well.
Mega cruise ships pass by.
The threat of more.

Then the unspoiled beach.
Seagulls caw, craving chips,
old slow thinkers walk and dip,
knowing dogs, strain on their leads
sniffing along the heritage path
as planes soar up, up and away
over the hidden gem of Yarra Bay.

$\mathcal{E}_C$

Unwrapping the Gift at Yarra Bay

Come the long drive along Anzac Parade
to a brand new playground made.
For family groups while leisure-makers,
lounge on sand, or leaf newspapers.

Breeze flowing fresh, gulls guzzling bread
and a rumpus of women, picnic rugs spread,
who neck bottles of beer, compare and contrast
cocktail ideas, and whose romance will last.

And all around red-wrapped native trees
festoon the paths in the southerly breeze,
paperbark, acacia, pigface, and samphire,
parade, stoic and full of seasonal cheer.

&c

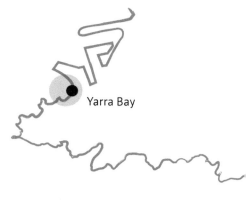

Yarra Bay

Sundays at La Perouse

Used to be
a tram line then
to Lapa
Sunday arvos
by tram or
a spin out there
in the Morris,
the small grey sedan
with seamed leather seats,
to see the Snake Man
perform snakey miracles
then bag the coiling
creatures
in his burlap bag, shoulder
his moving bounty and go;
and the Boomerang Man
performing miracles
of his own
his boomerang,
a small bent wooden piece
carved
and patterned with care.

We children marveled
at how he made it fly
spinning up and up
then turning on a sixpence
spinning back and back
to land somehow
exactly at his feet,
to smile briefly
at the applause
and invite a learner.
We children eager
but always too shy
never learned
the way of the boomerang,
the way of the
boomerang man.
His name I believe,
was Joe Timbery.

Congwong & Little Congwong

Secluded and unspoiled
these sibling beaches gaze out
at a changing Botany Bay.

Birds are drawn
to the rampant fringed bushland,
from magpie to currawong,
Pacific gull to soaring eagle;
hikers to fragrant bush tracks
from grevillia to bold banksia bloom
and a shy surprise of flannel flower;
divers to explore an underwater largesse,
nudists to go further seeking solitude,
families drawn to rock strewn sand,
safe jelly waves for kids.

At our lookout on a wild wet day
we sit here in sleety rain
watch through spattered glass, fixing on
a rare and pristine sight, two small beaches,
and the resilience of continuing
Aboriginal habitation.

LH

Frenchmans Beach
La Perouse Headland
Congwong Beach
Cruwee
Cove Beach

Bite-size Beaches

Two beaches scalloped from the coastal edge
as though bitten, munched by some sea giant
rocky outcrop connecting them like sisters:
Congwong Beach
the bigger, more accessible, more worldly
gives protection to its diminutive sister:
Little Congwong
shyly, tucked behind
a skirt of conglomerate boulders and slabs
perfect for exploring the natural world;
but beware the temptation
to scramble across the rocks,
of being drawn to this lesser beach
as rumour has it these rocks
protect sightseers from the nudists
who revel in the less is more
never caring for a bite of Eve's apple
content in celebrating their
liberation.

&c

The Friendship Poem

I walked with my friend
before the sun kissed the horizon
along the dappled leafy track
under the suspicious gazes of water skinks,
copper skinks and jacky dragons.
We walked and talked and laughed
until we reached Cruwee Cove Beach
with its many little rock pools.
There we sat and drank our flask of tea
perched on a rock
laughing at everything and nothing
munching biscuits
singing childhood ditties
as the day began
and time stood still here
with my friend.

Quoi de neuf?

La mystérieuse disparition du Comte de Lapérouse
qui arriva à Botany Bay seulement cinq jours après
le Capitaine Arthur Phillip; l'anglais.

Le Comte de Lapérouse
(en 1788 - mille sept cents quatre-vingts huit)
qui est arrivé à Botany Bay le 31 janvier
qui trouva les anglais déjà là
qui resta six semaines
qui partit le 10 mars
qui a disparu maintenant
avec l'équipage de son navire.

Louis XVI
à l'heure de sa mort
repensa au Comte de Lapérouse;
Et cria : *"Quoi de neuf?"*

Mais le mystère resta pendant
plus de quatre décennies
jusqu'à qu'un certain Capitaine
un Irelandais - Peter Dillon
 trouva l'évidence
de leur disparition
dans une tempête
sur un récif.

Jean-François de Galup
votre nom vi toujours
dans notre petit coin
du monde,
dans la belle baie
de La Pérouse.

LITTLE BAY

The Coast

i.   *on the green*
Two golfers pausing to converse
world matters, Covid, or the green.
Taking in the strutting magpies
strident black on pared down grass,
a calm swathe running to the verge
where nature still claims with its plunging edges.

ii.   *on the beach*
Lazy breakers, a lingering static flock
on wetted rocks
ascending, a single gull foolishly alone
skims and wheels and flutters a brief freedom
to a perfect landing in that stalwart crowd.

iii.   *by water and rock*
Swimmers, dippers, paddlers,
the sensualism of swimming
kayakers, waders, splashers all
picnickers and sandy pairs
birds picnicking too.

No thoughts on an earlier village here
sealed up from the outside world
for fifty years, a lazaret,
near this perfect little beach.

Long moments on carnival beach towels
an air of a throbbing summer calm
grey gatherings of pippis
in tiny perfect sculpted pools
the odd scuttler too.

iv.   *to the lighthouse*
I want a lighthouse
there at the rocky headland edge
to gleam delightedly white by day
and pulsate blinkingly by night
too far to reach...
like her lighthouse
the one that's never reached.

LH

Thoughts on a Tractor Driver

Little Bay, horseshoe bay of calm
where I float or swim with giant stingrays.
Cliff-top, a tractor trundling
makes me wonder
why the blue of the ocean
and the lunchtime hour
doesn't stop this driver from working,
won't halt the lights flashing,
or is it just me
who'd rather be in the sea?

Ec

Little Bay

Malabar Beach

Two Malabars

The silkiness of yellow sand,
splashing, piping children,
surfboards poised for unlikely waves,
canoes cutting smoothly, serenely
paddle boats gliding too.
Hard to imagine a cracking storm here,
a pounding surf and danger,
yet fishermen have gone here
from rocky vantage points,
disappeared into the swirl.
Five ships, one of them the Malabar,
came to grief here,
five shipwrecks in the indifferent Pacific
off the Malabar coastline.

The other Malabar,
another coastline edged
by the Arabian sea,
a history played out of long ago,
spice seekers and silk traders,
sea routes and silk roads.

A different history plays out here
at this tiny jewel beach,
a sacred ground,
Bora for the Bidjigal and the Gadigal
more ancient, and one
not smooth as silk.

LH

At Malabar

(with apologies to WB Yeats)

I will arise and go now, go to Malabar
and a familiar rock will I find there,
a blue bay will I have and salt coastline far,
and stay, not quite alone, free to think and stare.

And I shall have some peace, and more
for I find peace by this sea,
washing, washing on this shore
and speaking, speaking calm to me.

LH

Malabar Beach

The Quiet Beach at Malabar

(more apologies to WB Yeats)

I will arise and go now, and go to Malabar
and a little boat launch there, of wood with calico sails.
Port holes will I have brass-rimmed, a cabin for the rain
and live on rippling Malabar Bay, peaceful once again.

I shall relish the quiet pace there
for my calmer mind to grow,
days gently passing in a range of blues
noon bright to inky light, all changes slow.

Ec

MAROUBRA BEACH

I hurry to see the rising sun

The path which leads me to the beach
curves and dips
its criss-crossed moulded plastic sheets
hurt as they press against my bare feet.
From the small crest of this path
I see the beach pre-dawn.
When I reach the sand
a slash of light scores the dark sky;
as I dump my bag and towel
light cuts through the clouds.

Here comes the sun,
resplendent Maroubra Bay!

Rip-swept

Maroubra beach break
warm tide, carry me to shore!
I gasp, rip-swept south.

Ɛc

Maroubra Beach

A long-ago day at the...

A gaggle of
Maroubra kids
we take the tram
from the Junction
right to the beach,
trail the hot sand
with drawstring
beach bags,
spread skimpy towels,
waste no time
paddling, wading,
building sand things
with the little ones.

Then the surfing
out the back,
spread-eagled
on an undulating surface.
A fear-edged return
through the breakers,
more dalliances in and out
until big sister says
it's time.

The gathering up,
making a straggly line
to the fish'n chip shop
out of the still hot sun.
A swarm of freckled kids
salt encrusted lashes
and lips
waiting good naturedly,
for the butcher's paper cone,
hot chips, salt encrusted,
outer wrapped in
yesterday's news.

Making for the tram shed
slowly savouring
chip by precious chip,
as the next tram rolls in,
waits for the gaggle of
them, sunburnt kids
who board and make
their sandy, blistery,
satisfied return.

The Surfer's Lament

The wave was so good
I almost had it mate.
I took it too soon!
I rode it too late!

The Boys from the Surf

Ink-etched bodies
on salt-washed boards
smiling through green waves
rising on foam crests
now riding like demons
a bare-backed cavalcade
these princes of pipelines
enveloped in the channels
of the break and the roll
step off pronto
wade through the wash
their grins deep as the ocean
beaming wide as the bay
flicking wet locks
boards braced under arms
the boys from the surf
dripping breathless
a reckless freedom is found.

Mahon Pool

Scattered clumps of daisies in the grass,
a modest 'splendour' this spring day,
and clumps of people passing down the path;
prams and surfboards, bikes and pushers
and the old ones with their canes,
hand-held babies, rampaging kids
drawn like us to edges,
briefly reverential,
whole moments to watch the spectacle
sea beating its way in and in
waves veined in ragged white
waves colliding creating rising and rising,
a maelstrom of foam spume and spray,
rising and rising then walloping
worn walls of sandstone, and walloping again,
spuming over clumped rocks
waves pulsing through the pool
cries of squeaky glee,
the triumph and the pleasure
being wave borne, foam encircled,
memories of the child back then.

So strong, so bright, the childhood hour.

'Though nothing can bring back the hour
Of splendour in the grass
Of glory in the flower,
We will grieve not, rather find
Strength in what remains behind.'

- Wordsworth-

Ladies' Baths

The entrance to Ladies' Baths
forbidden, forgotten,
unknown to men.

Beyond the gate
coins dropped
or placed on the shiny counter.
The question of where to sit
easily answered.

Sloped grassy verges
hold-on places, rough and folded,
flat or not so flat rocks
but safe havens all.

Breasts bared or bodies fully covered
down slippery pool steps, we
plunge

    plunge

       plunge

into the depths
of a space and a history,
birthing rights,
once babies delivered here.

Breathe freely now
in the grace of knowing
we are woman.

ℇ*c*

Wylie's Baths

Miss Mina Wylie taught me to swim here,
the tidal pool that harbours living things.
Miss Mina Wylie, thickset and old, but
medal winner at the Stockholm Games!
among first women Olympic swimmers.
She stood resplendent in her navy Speedos
at the edge of the seawater baths
where sea urchins and other spikey things clung,
where my beating heart surely must be heard,
after face-in-the-water drill
hands safely clutching the rocks;
Miss Mina Wylie in those no-frill swimmers
demonstrating so smoothly from the edge
the way my childish arms
should move through deeper water.
Face down like this, arms in and out like this,
Now go! Terrified I struck out.
I swam!

Giles Baths: the Boy who Floats

He floats, eyes open, splayed across
the tippy tops of gurgling waves,
splashing over the rock wall.
A puffy little white cloud shifts shape.
Above, on the cliffs, Sunday walkers
watch for passing pods of whales.
Can he hear his heart through the water
or know when the next kid will dive-bomb?
A passing swimmer spoils his reverie.
The boy stands up knee deep,
his foot is pierced, his eyes blind with tears,
an urchin broken, a boy in pain,
the boy who floats
no more.

&c

McIver Ladies' Baths

A tidal pool sheltered
against the cliff face
known to be a special birthing place for
First Women here long, long ago.
Despite remonstrations and discrimination bills
it still remains exclusive
for women and babies, for girls
only.

LH

Sisterhood

A silver coin,
entitled female gaze
long, strong,
beckons all women
one sisterhood
beyond discrimination.
Our blood bond, our glorious feminism
unties yet unites us
at the Ladies' Baths.
The sun's rays warm our skin,
the rocks, the water, the women
at McIver Ladies' Baths.

COOGEE BEACH

Piece of Cake

*Twice a year, Coogee Surf Club hosts a swim challenge
around Wedding Cake Island, a distance of about
2.4 km. Throughout ANZAC Day, local surfers honour
fallen war heroes by paddling out to the island.*

A chain of water safety crews,
a necklace of colourful surfboards,
perfect conditions; a piece of cake!
White-iced, low-lying, rocky outcrop
shell-adorned rocks,
dampen the spirited swells.
Beach protector, destination, pretty picture.
So familiar, well established
an event in Coogee's calendar
and now about to take the challenge;
Stomachs lurch, mouths dry, hearts pound.
The starter's whistle shrills,
competitors run and dive,
each wanting their piece of cake,
their piece of Wedding Cake Island.

The Reef at Coogee Beach

Today I swim towards the reef
through the whitewash and its sandy spills
into the clear stillness out the back.
The reef's curves guide my circuit
past underwater nooks and nests
where shells rock and fish sleep.
around and back, now shore bound
I cut through glassy water
the limey seagrass sways its sassy shape
beckoning with hula strands of joy.
As if to celebrate my passage,
a simultaneous rise of silver dollar sprats
drift in unison up from scraggy seaweed
to greet me, then turn as one and are gone.

&c

View from Dolphin Point

Another sweeping view of Coogee Beach
from Wylie's Baths to the Pavilion,
once the Aquarium Pool
with its high domed roof,
part of the Coogee Palace.
Hard to imagine a pier, a pleasure park
with whirligigs and toboggan rides,
a bandstand and an aviary
now a high domed eatery
of splendid proportions
beside a quiet park.
Homage on the way up
through this park
to the lookouts over Coogee;
a seat for a painter
who captured earlier times;
a looped steel memorial
that tells its shocking story;
then up along the cliff tops
the looking out and out,
the breaking away...

LH

The Dawn

The night sky is not so dark by the sea.
At the beach on the sand before the dawn
pinpoint lights curve by the esplanade
an orange glow mirrored on the pavers.
The night rain has paused
leaving only the waves to splash the shore.
I step, each rainbow step a reminder of pride,
my feet crunching on rain-crusted top-sand.
Out on the horizon, a fishing boat outlined
with its blinking lonely light, bobs and sways.
This dark is not dark.
From the sandy bay houses nestled into the hillside,
the squares of light from myriad windows
keep dark at bay.

Coogee's night fading.
Ever pinkening stripes of cloud reveal
shapes of other feet, show other trails,
not alone, not dark.
Following those prints,
in between the time of night and day.
sand giving way beneath my toes,
I run.

&c

On the Path at Dolphin Point

Metropolis
by sand and sea
where cross-topped steeples rise
where domes of blue and white
on top of arched windowpanes rest.

Coogee's planted pride
lavender clumps
native rosemary
Norfolk pines
all accommodate the wind.

From Dolphin Point to Ladies' Baths
from crescent steps to bay side splashes
Coogee's tourist-crowded beach
infiltrates like sand,
or a mighty rush of waves.

&c

Coogee Beach

GORDON'S BAY

Splendid Fairy Wren

Your name
says it all
sight
sound
movement
come together,
my spirit lifts its wings,
takes flight.

In a flash of blue
I'll follow you,
your presence
as ethereal as your name.
Little wren
you bring me joy.

To think each diminutive feather,
each claw, your fruit-pip eyes,
minute heart and lungs
are so delicately crafted.
Your size and fragile beauty
have the power to move me,
to hold me to the spot
captivated every time,
tiny, glorious,
splendid fairy wren.

&c

Unexpected Greeting

Running up hill
towards the overlook
I spy a honey eater in the bush
sitting still
though its golden breast
betrays it.

Preposterous little bird
hello! I see you!
you are perfect!
so independent.
so aware.
so free.

Ec

Gordon's Bay

The Yellow Breasted Honeyeater

Flash of yellow
a spying eye
this small bird sees me
as I walk by
it blinks as I near
its chirping stops
it winks at me
from its nest
deep in the bush on the cliff

Birds on a Rock Platform

30 white birds synchronise
their white fluttering lift-off,
30 little hearts must beat so fast,
30 little bodies tilt into the wind
to be airborne so perfectly together.
Startled apart they make line formations,
wide wheeling clever arcs again and again.
An invisible sign and as one
they land on the wide rock platform
to mew and call, to scrabble,
30 scavenger gulls again.

In Memoriam

Pausing here
on the 'in memoriam' seat
the seat for the man and his son
fringed by hardy coastal scrub,
I watch.
A path curves by
a welter of kids on bikes,
the dog walkers, the lovers,
the strollers, the intent joggers,
lifetimes unfolding at Clovelly Beach.
The sea, the grey heavenly clouds,
a perfect place for death and life.

The Bench

Here on the bench
I say your name
though I didn't know you.
Dates etched on the wood,
your birth, your death.
These are historic, unchanging.
Time keeps moving,
the birds keep singing
yet you are present here.

Dogs on Parade

haiku

Dogs on tight leashes
ever straining to escape
plodding human pace.

LH

Clouds over Clovelly

haiku

Strange to contemplate
each every moving cloudscape
forms drifts only once.

LH

Many Moods

Being at Clovelly Beach
where nature's rare lightshow
shifts through midnight water
spilling phosphorescence
or in the heat of a summer's day
catches the sun's rays
radiating in diamond splattered shafts,
the water's brilliance in my eyes.

How is one day so different from the next
and yet the same in this sparkling,
rocking, lapping, treacherous bay?
The rough waves might reach to grasp my limbs
to draw and tumble me around,
other times enticing me to float
languid amongst armfuls of tropical fish
contemplating the pleasure
of being just here.

Ec

Stalling the Weather

Guaranteed darkening clouds steal light,
birds with their perpetual songs,
children with their endless mirth.
Though it isn't certain, I'll bet on rain later
so take my chance
to sit a while longer
and read a bit longer.

ℰℭ

The Understudy

Clovelly Beach,
a strange narrow reaching inlet,
concrete flanks, chained steps,
subterranean theatre.
A mecca to crowds of swimmers,
prime viewing
to the dress circle of the reef.
All are ushered
for the show-stopping glamour of fish
who sashay along this underwater stage.
A player, one of Bluey's descendants,
another "Elvis of the Sea"
comes into the spotlight,
bows down to grasp a sea urchin. Star act!
Whilst in the wings
stealthy between the rocky recesses
a Port Jackson shark glides by,
makes its way to somewhere else.

ε_C

Clovelly Beach

WAVERLEY CEMETERY

Standing at the Cemetery

Sandstone gully
ocean lapping down below
between heavens and the deep
top heavy with marble headstones
history laden.
Gazing upon these names and places
these sinking, forgotten, crumbling graves,
I wonder about their residents...

A wave crashes
drawing my eyes
towards the skyline
beyond which home
and other marvellous lands lie hidden.
My history, my dreams stirring.
Cruise and cargo ships drift,
tiny on the horizon,
parallel lives continuing.

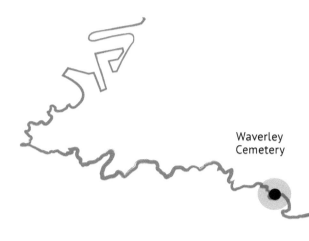

Waverley
Cemetery

A Sea Song in Remembrance of John

In his arms lying in softest water,
the crowning sky the arc of paler blue
allowing all the sun there is,
in his arms, her arms entwined,
feet pointing down,
all the fishes in the world
all the caves and corals
and all the altering depths
there at her feet,
her pointing down feet.

In his arms lying in softest water,
out there, out there beyond the waves,
beyond the bathers too,
laughing and calling,
rising and falling in his arms,
in that gentle, swelling, fathomless place,
watchful with such salt-rimmed eyes
of each other, in that profound sea,
only two, the only two becalmed,
in a shining world without horizon.

LH

CLIFF BOARDWALK

from Waverley to Bronte

The Hanging Swamp

The wash,
the shh-shh-shh of the wash
up here,
the endless wash underscoring meditations.
The hanging swamp not far below,
a hanging cliff side garden.
Not the smooth limestone of Nebuchadnezzar's build
for his homesick wife longing for the greens of Persia,
but nature's sandstone cliffs, perfect golden chunks
with crevices, fissures and clefts.
Not gardens of olive, oak and pomegranate,
nor pines and cypress, quince or myrrh
but banksia, melaleuca and coastal tea tree;
a hanging swamp, pockets of rainwater,
for mosses and lichens, sedges and grasses
and the striped march frogs, *tok tok.*
and the common eastern froglets, *crik-crik crik.*
Not aqueducts and sluice gates,
but marvels of nature's engineering
older than Babylon, primordial,
an ancient terrestrial landscape
still weathering, still changing
to the shh-shh-shh of the wash
the endless shh-shh-shh
of the wash.

LH

Mindful

Please be mindful
The painted sign exhorts
Of jagged edges
Of errant waves

please be mindful
of restless sea
and flowering weeds
and all this flagrant
coastal splendour

LH

Cliff boardwalk

Bogey Hole (i)

Late afternoon swims in still warm shadows,
fish and chips in sandy four-berth shelters,
strumpet birds pacing to and fro,
a child striking out across the bogey hole,
the olds safe in its rock-bound swell,
real surfers escaping outside to the wild surf,
and then their balletic board rides
on carefully chosen waves.
Exaltation in hips and shoulders and guiding arms
to shore, and admiring eyes,
here, safe and envious in the Bogey Hole.

Bogey Hole (ii)

Once we swam in the Bogey Hole with you,
two friends, suggesting you run away
from the place that had you in its maw.
'Don't go back,' we said. 'Ever' we said
but the chemo called and you knew
your strength was ebbing like the tide
and you went with the sound of the sea,
the tang, the force, the frightfulness
companioning you.

LH

Bronte Beach

The Bogey Hole

Waves hopscotch on rocks
Holding safe the swimmers
The dippers the toe-tippers
Cold and warm
Old and young
Corralled and cleansed
White on blue
Dark corners light edges
Shallow to deep
In and out
Of Bronte's Bogey Hole.

Ec

Tamarama Beach

Sea Gazing

Tamarama Tamarama,
Gama Gama meaning storm,
good to sound your name.

Once this little wild beach
had creek water
running from a waterfall
through the gully
across the beach
into a sand channel
skipping to the sea.

It was later tamed,
with pipes, a tunnel,
uglified with a funfair,
a fun ride, cliff to cliff
as if the waves
not fun enough.

Someone saw sense
and it was dismantled,
the beach resuming itself
yet slowly buildings appeared
against its golden sandstone rockface
tucked in and streamlined.

Only the perfect
swathe of yellow sand
running freely
between rugged cliff edges
to a restless water's edge
stays jubilantly the same.

LH

The Lifeguard's Outpost

Door open
duty calls
green wetsuit hanging
it should be lifeguard red!

Seaside Palette

I want to paint this sea
creamy eggshell greys and blues.
Up pops a surfboard neon green
intruding.

The Boogie Boarder

Backwards she flops
flipping flippered feet
and twists
landing on her boogie board.
I've lost her now
where is she?
Up she comes
the other side of the waves
too close to the rocks.
Waves drag and form to meet her
gathering her up in shades of green
thrusting her to shore.

At Tama

haiku

'Waves running, Gangi?'
Checked daily at her window
for surfer grandsons

LH

Sculptures by the Sea

haiku

Pacific perfect
sculptures fixed on sand and cliff
joyful offerings

LH

Tamarama Beach

MACKENZIES BEACH

Mackenzies Beach (i)

haiku

Jagged rocks are bare
heft and hump of sand and there
once again a beach!

LH

Mackenzies Beach (ii)

haiku

Azure lace ocean
mystical Mackenzies beach
once in seven years.

Ec

Disappearing Beach

Path twisting
      stepping
            sea-bound

Grass bush flax
      flat rocks
            tides swell

Hidden beach
      revealed
            only now

&c

Mackenzies Beach

Arise, Mackenzies Beach!

Underwater treasure
heaving rocks upon rocks
half-dragged out of the water
like some gin-soaked, half-drowned,
drunken sailor sprawled motionless
left at the mercy of slapping waves
until the moon tide and the seasons collide
in a terrestrial alignment
and out of the depths arises
Mackenzies Beach.

εc

The Afternoon of the Pervert

Funny that it should be the afternoon of the pervert
because we are exposing our thoughts
in an unguarded way to one another
on that dramatic cliff walk,
Tamarama to Bondi,
and he was such an ineffectual
pale skinned man, redheaded,
in teal blue shimmery bathers,
a thin gingery face.

There in that lonely minute
her thoughts were spilling out,
uncertainties, anxieties
about the man we knew so well
and the sudden shock of the pale uncovered body
jumped us into panic.

Girl-like, woman-like
I had imagined her composure
yet it was she who cried,
she who cried and I who comforted
though my words were sharp with fear.

Now with these years gone
I am clutched at by another fear,
not for the man who was there
gesticulating wildly
who loses all menace with the passing of time,
not for him but for the man who wasn't there
on that summer windy afternoon
among the words that blew around
like flowers on the wind for him,
whose silence encloses him
in prison of years.

Running up the hill towards Mackenzies Point

(Apologies to Kate Bush)

Without barricades or fences
the uphill path
towards the turret
challenges me.
What would it be like
to fly?

BONDI BEACH

Bondi Beach (i)

haiku

Utmost sand, sea, sky,
hard not to be astounded,
again and again.

LH

Bondi Beach (ii)

haiku

Bodies in the surf,
sun-languid watchers, only
dream of riding waves.

LH

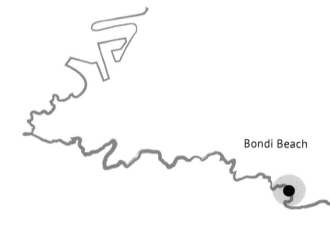

Bondi Beach

Bondi Pavilion

Pavilion of schemes and changing dreams,
graceful build on sand, welcoming Pacific weathers,
all moods and changes, plans and abandonments,
a building up and wearing down, a stolid waiting game,
revered, neglected, saved time and again,
for reinventions.

First a castle-like structure for dressing sheds
with its fairytale turrets circa 1911,
a place to hide the shame
of wanton changing on the beach,
1000 wooden change boxes, complete with books,
a concerned Council lent for reading!
Then a reinvention.
A world-wide contest 1923, and re-design.
Born, a 'Mediterranean colonnade'
theatre and galleries, tourist shops
Turkish baths, a restaurant and a ballroom.

Space leased out, 1933.
The slide, rooms deteriorating
until a war brought new use,
the American Red Cross
and American Officers' Club, 1944,
Surf and Dance late forties, proceeds
for the Digger's Cigarette Fund.

More years of disparate neglect until
The Bondi Theatre Group with
the Waverley Council, 1973
began a transformation
'from a damp mildewed, mock-Spanish mansion'
to cultural and community centre.
New theatre, exhibition rooms, courtyards
an amphitheatre, a child care centre,
craft workshops, an art gallery.

Once boldly called *Playground of the Pacific*
now refurbished and replanned,
the graceful build prevails,
for the sandy footed surfers,
the flaneurs, the tourists, the locals,
for community, a heritage piece forever.
Pavilion of schemes and changing dreams.

LH

Bondi Beach Supreme

Your moods flow as ours,
as the push and pull of tides.
Faces to the wind,
waves to the beach,
horizon to vast sky,
ours for the looking.
The bathers, the surfers, the board riders,
the watchers, the listeners, the learners,
the mish-mash of the sun adoring
strewn across pale sand.

The dip, the plunge, the shock, the dream.
Timeless exuberance, Bondi Beach supreme.

The Bikini Wars

The bikini
named for the Bikini Atoll
a bombshell of another kind.

Some Bondi Beach inspectors enjoyed the job
measuring offending bikinis, and if too small,
ordering offending women off the beach,
so that, 'dignity and moral order is restored.'
Local Government Ordinance, No 52
the press agog and eager to recount bikini wars.

From no bathing until after dark
to neck to knee costumes
or garments that hid the female form,
all the way to string and thong bikinis
a long explosive history.

4th century Roman women
wore bikini garments for exercise,
mosaics tell.
Our mermaid swimmer, Annette Kellerman,
first woman to wear a one piece,
displayed her offending legs.
Arrested in Boston in the early 1900s
for immodest attire,
she inspired global fashionistas to change.
Yet on Australian beaches, bikinis
outlawed for more than fifty years.

The swinging sixties and hosts of women
bikini clad on Bondi Beach,
too few inspectors,
and unwilling lifeguards
Waverley's Local Government Ordinance, No 52.
looking foolish, was revoked.
String bikini, retro Y thong or cheeky bottom
the bikini wars were over.

LH

City to Surf

Colour-coded runners cascade surf-bound.
Expressway of sweat and euphoria
Stretching out in motley form
Along Rushcutters Bay
Sweeping towards New South Head Road.
Then up, up, up Heartbreak Hill
Still only half-way!

Greeted by water-bearing scouts
And cheering crowds
The pumped-up throng of athletes
Chicane-ing onto Military Rd
With lactic-ladened limbs
Before the breathless blast to Bondi Beach
The final kilometre, the trial over.

The triumph, the time.

Lifesaver

Red and yellow skull-capped patrols
All squinting eyes, strong stances
With colour-matching safety tubes
Tucked under arms
Survey the surf
At the ready.

North Bondi

What are the Wild Waves Saying?

This is based on a Victorian conversation poem written by John Glover in 1859.

What are the wild waves saying?
They surge, they churn and they roar
and a voice inside keeps urging me
calling me from this shore...

Brother, hear these crashing waves,
their rhythm as they roll,
breathe deeply as they rise
exhale slowly as they fall.

I hear your calming words,
this breath could help, it's true,
but there's such darkness in my mind,
oh! Sister what shall I do?

Come sit with me a while,
together let's talk it through
with senses five and our two minds
I am here with you.

Sister, your just being here,
it calms my troubled mind,
understanding all you ask of me
brings a song of a different kind.

Brother yes, it's a song of hope,
just as light follows dark,
just as waves keep rolling in
these glimmers help make a fresh start.

Yes, yes, I'm hearing that now,
nature sings as she has ever done,
an ancient song, now a calming song
reassuring me sister, that perhaps I belong.

LH &c

North Bondi

The Dancer

Thumpy bumpy music
from the ice cream truck
shatters the sounds of sea
surfers' cries or bird calls
as she dances her fey little dance
on the tar, the big lass
with the multi-coloured thighs
in the too tight tights
and the too loud sounds.
Happy in the clatter
and the swoop and dive
in the thrall of her body freedom,
the clouds swan free too,
ample trails over Bondi Beach heavens,
the waves repeat and repeat their charter
as she dances, in her own sweet sphere,
as she dances oblivious
to all but music's strokes.

LH

My Surfer

A tribute to Judith Wright's depiction of a surfer in her poem The Surfer.

My surfer is a little dot
rising up out of the effervesce
to disappear again
as she is thrust down
in Judith's *hollow and coil*
the energy is made
transferred, discharged
with the *grey-wolf* sea
as she negotiates her passage
  below

    unseen

      unheard

       through
the crashing, the roar, the growl;
such crescendo –
as if applauding my surfer,
on her podium of a board
as she pops back up
on the crest of the next wave
riding high.

Ec

Watson's Bay

Watson's Bay Seascape

Fly down the hill to Watson's Bay
past the stalwart lighthouses
to a seascape wide, generous,
liberal chunky cliffs to tiny beaches,
to harbour glimpses and beyond.
Alpha and omega here
almost too vast to catch in words,
this shining beauty to be had,
a seascape beguiling,
both worldly and divine.

LH

Watson's Bay

The Lookout

haiku

Grey tilted ledges
Exposed thrust up skyward-bound
Janus-faced lookout

The Gap

The cliff's stern prow
the sea's chewed remorselessly,
a disparate tree clings,
thrashes, holds on
despite ill winds.

Runners coming up
the rising winding path
to reach the vantage point
and soaring views
of cliff fall, and
the fullest spectacle of sea,
to pause, heaving then,
sucking in the small triumph
of up here;
and yet
unable to uncouple all
thoughts
of other frantic feet
desperate to find their way
and finding their desperate way
up here.

LH

Roll on, thou deep and dark blue ocean — roll!

Roll on, thou green and glistering sea — roll!
Roll on, thou great and growing ocean — roll!

Photo Matt Hardy, unsplash.com

Poets

Libby Hathorn

Libby Hathorn is a prolific writer, poet and librettist. She has received many awards over her long career, most recently the ABIA, Pixie O'Harris Award, 2022, and the Lady Cutler Award, 2021, both for services to children's literature. She and her daughter Lisa, won the CBCA Picture Book of the Year Award, Younger Readers, 2021 for *No! Never!* (Hachette). She lives and works in Sydney.

libbyhathorn.com

Elizabeth Cummings

Coogee based, Elizabeth was born in England grew up in Scotland. Having spent many years teaching in the UK and New Zealand, Elizabeth now works in the mental health sector. In 2015, she won the South Coast Writers Prize for a poem on gender identity. In 2022, Elizabeth's mental health narratives were translated into a Lithuanian language puppet play by the Kaunas State Puppet theatre.

elizabethmarycummings.com

${\mathcal{A}}$CKNOWLEDGEMENTS

p12   Libby has based her final line on the last line of the poet Dorothea Mackellar's poem *My Country* as an ending for her poem, *Singing the Coast*.

p24   *Quoi de Neuf?* was inspired by a question that was said to have been asked by Louis XVI as he was being led to the guillotine. Editor in translation, Delphine Banse.

p26   Libby has made reference to the title of her novel, *To the Lighthouse* by Virginia Woolf, in her poem *The Coast iv. to the lighthouse*.

p31 & 32 Libby and Elizabeth have modelled their poems on *The Lake Isle of Innisfree* by William Yeats, inspiration for their poems about Malabar.

p34 Elizabeth used the line from the lyrics *Here Comes the Sun* by the Beatles, as inspiration for her poem *I hurry to see the rising sun*.

p40   Libby has quoted five lines from William Wordsworth's poem *The Splendour in the Grass* as an addendum to her poem *Mahon Pool*, Maroubra.

p41   Elizabeth's line 'We are Woman' was inspired by the lyric 'I am Woman' by Helen Reddy as inspiration for her poem *Ladies' Baths*.

p66   Libby's poem *In His Arms* was first published in *Heard Singing* (Out of India Press) 2000.

p70   Libby's Poem *The Hanging Swamp* was first published in *Women's Ink!* magazine, Summer 2022.

p87   Libby Hathorn *The Afternoon of the Pervert* first published in *Mother I'm Rooted*, Outback Press, 1975.

p90   A version of *Bondi Beach haiku* was first published in *Mother Earth*, Hachette, 2023.

p100   Libby and Elizabeth based *What are the Wild Waves Saying?* on a Victorian conversation poem by John Glover (1813-1870) which was set to music as a duet for soprano and tenor.
NB: It is known that the practice of mindfulness such as guided breathing and five sense awareness helps harmonize body and mind.

p103   Elizabeth was inspired in her poem *My Surfer* by Judith Wright's poem *The Surfer*.

p107   *Roll on, thou deep and dark blue ocean — roll!* is an excerpt from *Childe Harold's Pilgrimage* by Lord Byron (1788-1824).